Reality of Banking and International Monetary Systems

Curse or Comfort for the Mankind!

But those who **devour interest** (usury) become like the one whom Satan has bewitched and maddened by his touch. They have been condemned to this condition because they say, "Trade is just like interest", whereas **Allah has made trade lawful and interest unlawful**. Henceforth, if one abstains from taking interest after receiving this admonition from his Lord, no legal action will be taken against him regarding the interest he had devoured before; his case shall ultimately go to Allah. But if one repeats the same crime after this, he shall go to Hell, where he shall abide for ever.

Al Quran: Chapter 2, Verse 275

O Allah! show us the truth as true and inspire us to follow it

Show us falsehood as falsehood, and inspire us to abstain from it

Ameen Ya Rab Al A'alameen!

I am also indebted and grateful to my respected teachers, Sheikh Imran Nazar Hossein, Mike Maloney, Edward G. Griffin and Jim Rickards, who are the source of knowledge and motivation for me and enabled me to put up this humble effort!

May Allah SWT accept my efforts for enlightening and safeguarding the humanity in the Current Age of Deception i.e. Fitan (End Times) –

Ameen Ya Rab Al A'alameen!

CONTENTS

PREFACE

This humble effort is done to educate the people (common / learned), especially those **who intend to seek** "knowledge / Truth" about the **Banking and Monetary Systems**, which govern our daily lives. There are some critical concepts and their implications related to currency and money, which in my experience, even the well-educated people are also unaware of!

I have tried to cover the **historical background** of the "**modern banking and monetary systems**" concisely, so that reader may **have a fair idea** quickly about how they all started, what happened and where they are leading the mankind!

I have also tried to identify the **group behind the banking industry** (with evidence) and **their ulterior motives** for the mankind, so the people may be aware of the **critical situation and try to safeguard themselves, families and friends!** I have also **suggested solutions to "pinching issue of mortgage-based loans"** for the people living in Western societies!

The book also covers future of monetary system and its repercussions for the mankind!

I have also presented a **case study**, covering **conventional and Islamic banking systems in Pakistan**. This will **clarify several concepts** about the Islamic Banking in a simplified manner to the respected reader. Finally, the **conclusion is of prime importance** for the reader!

HISTORICAL BACKGROUND

EMERGENCE OF MODERN BANKING

It is important to learn some authentic historical background about the "modern banking system" before establishing an opinion and arriving at   Truth!

- **Bank of England** established - **1694**

- England's crushing defeat by France, the dominant naval power, in naval engagements culminating in the 1690 Battle of Beachy Head, became the catalyst for England's rebuilding itself as a global power. England had no choice but to build a powerful navy. No public funds were available, and the credit of William III's government was so low in London that it was impossible for it to borrow the £1,200,000 (at 8% p.a.) that the government wanted.

- William Paterson proposed a loan of **£1.2m** to the government; in return the subscribers would be incorporated as **The Governor and Company of the Bank of England** with <u>long-term banking privileges including the issue of notes.</u> The Royal Charter was granted on 27 July through the passage of the Tonnage Act 1694. Public finances were in so dire a condition at the time that the terms of the loan were that it was to be serviced at a rate of **8% per annum**, and there was also a service charge of **£4,000 per annum for the management of the loan.**

1694 Banknote of Bank of England

Meyer Amchel Rothschild said:

"Let me issue and control a nation's money, and I care not who writes its laws"

(1743-1812)

In 1773, Rothschild, formerly Bauer, pulled together 12 other investors to join in his plan to dominate the world. On May 1, 1776, Adam Weishaupt (brainchild of Order of Illuminati) retained by Rothschild's completed their world dominance plan.

FAMOUS PERSONALITIES - ABOUT THE BANKING AND MONETARY SYSTEMS

These bankers financed the wars and revolutions (American, French & Bolshevik) - ROTHSCHILD are behind all wars / revolutions since Napoleon, as they found it to be profitable to finance both sides of the war!

Reference: The Elite, the 'Great Game', & World War III

http://www.newdawnmagazine.com/articles/the-elite-the-great-game-world-war-iii   By: Prof Dr. Mujahid Kamran, VC Punjab University

In 1849, Guttle Schnapper, the wife of Mayer Amschel (Rothschild) stated: "If my sons did not want wars, there would be none."

In **1835, US President Andrew Jackson** declared his disregard for the international bankers: **"You are a den of vipers. I intend to rout you out, and by the Eternal God, I will rout you out. If the people only understood the rank injustice of our money and banking system, there would be a revolution before morning."**

Secretary of State Thomas Jefferson (subsequently US President) was adamantly opposed to the idea of a privately owned federal bank and said: "I sincerely believe the banking institutions having the issuing power of money are more

dangerous to liberty than standing armies" "the principle of spending money to be paid by prosperity under the name of funding is but swindling futurity on a large scale". If the American people ever allow the banks to control the issuance of their currency. the banks and corporations that will grow up around them will deprive the people of all property, until their children wake up homeless on the continent their fathers conquered.

Henry Ford once said, "It is well enough that people of the nation do not understand our banking and monetary system, for if they did, I believe there would be a revolution before tomorrow morning".

CREATION OF FEDERAL RESERVE BANK (USA)

Federal Reserve is generally a government entity that frustrated high schoolers in America (and worldwide) are forced to learn about before entering adulthood and forgetting exactly **what it is or why it exists?** The Fed is the central banking system that was created at the tail end of 1913 as **a response to a string of financial crises**.

It is responsible for implementing the United States' monetary policy! It's all boring (though hugely consequential) stuff. The Fed doesn't bomb anything, invade anything, or even tax anything.

But!

One of the most influential and popular documents pushing this tale is 1994's "The Creature from Jekyll Island", written by author Edward Griffin. discloses the **secret agenda behind the Fed's creation** and its complicity in atrocity (financial or otherwise), the book soon, which took off as a best-seller.

It recounts a secret meeting that took place in 1910 on Jekyll Island, a stretch of white-sand beaches and beautiful landscape off the coast of

Georgia. It was an exclusive boys-club gathering of American financiers and politicians who wanted to draft a monetary policy to favour the few and eventually enslave the humanity!

The meeting spawned the draft legislation for the creation of the central bank. Griffin spins this trip to Jekyll Island as the birthplace of the nefarious, scary, all-powerful banking system that every decent American should want torn down immediately.

The whole thing reads like a thriller, as well as an amateur polemic.

"The Fed has become an accomplice in the support of totalitarian regimes throughout the world," he writes. **"As stated at the beginning of this study, that is one of the reasons it should be abolished: It is an instrument of totalitarianism."**

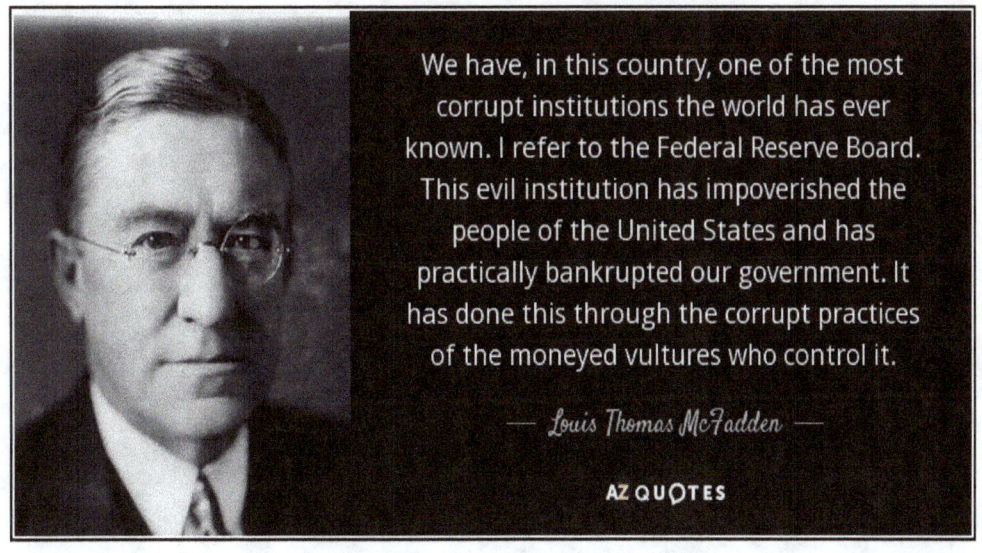

We have, in this country, one of the most corrupt institutions the world has ever known. I refer to the Federal Reserve Board. This evil institution has impoverished the people of the United States and has practically bankrupted our government. It has done this through the corrupt practices of the moneyed vultures who control it.

— *Louis Thomas McFadden* —

AZ QUOTES

The Federal Reserve Bank is a consortium of <u>twelve private banks</u> which are not part of the United States Government.

The Primary Owners of the Federal Reserve Bank Are:

1. **Rothschild's of London and Berlin**
2. **Lazard Brothers of Paris**
3. **Israel Moses Seaf of Italy**
4. **Kuhn, Loeb & Co. of Germany, and New York**
5. **Warburg & Company of Hamburg, Germany**
6. **Lehman Brothers of New York**
7. **Goldman, Sachs of New York**
8. **Rockefeller Brothers of New York**

I care not what puppet is placed upon the throne of England to rule the Empire on which the sun never sets.

The man who controls Britain's money supply controls the British Empire, and I control the British money supply.

-Nathan Rothschild

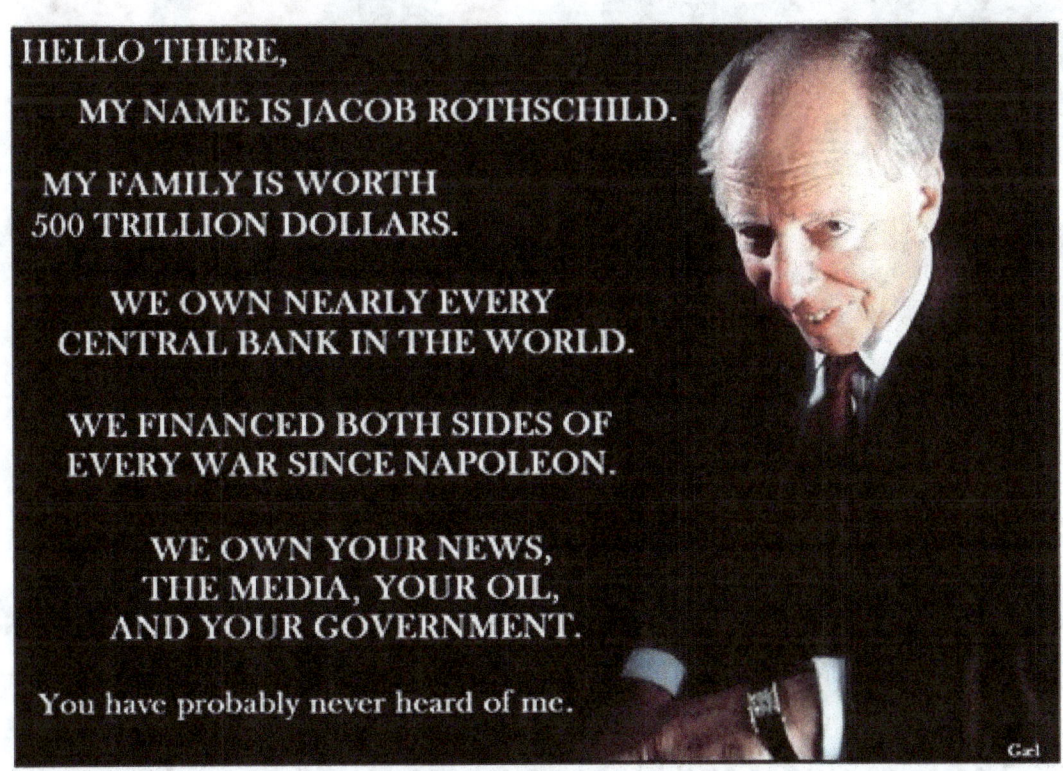

HELLO THERE,

MY NAME IS JACOB ROTHSCHILD.

MY FAMILY IS WORTH
500 TRILLION DOLLARS.

WE OWN NEARLY EVERY
CENTRAL BANK IN THE WORLD.

WE FINANCED BOTH SIDES OF
EVERY WAR SINCE NAPOLEON.

WE OWN YOUR NEWS,
THE MEDIA, YOUR OIL,
AND YOUR GOVERNMENT.

You have probably never heard of me.

Gæl

HOW BANKING SYSTEM WORKS?

Authority to print currency!

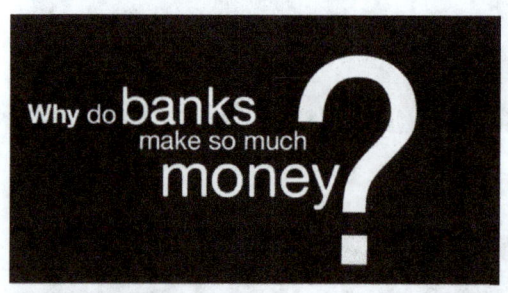

They lend money, created out of nothing, as DEBT and charge interest!!!

They get bigger and bigger over the Debt based System!!

They get bigger and bigger over the Debt based System!!

They now can print as much they can!!

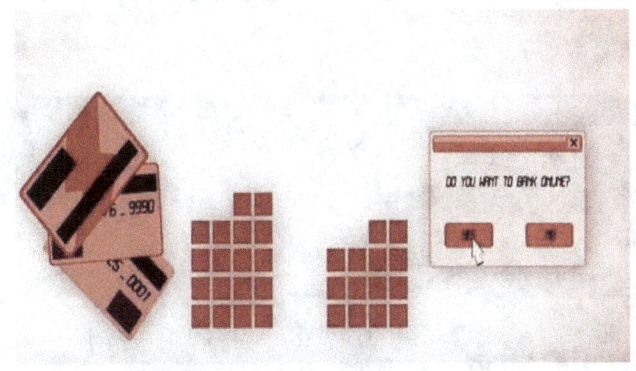

Paper Money, Plastic / Digital Money

Today, 97% is Digital Money

They control the global money supply and finances

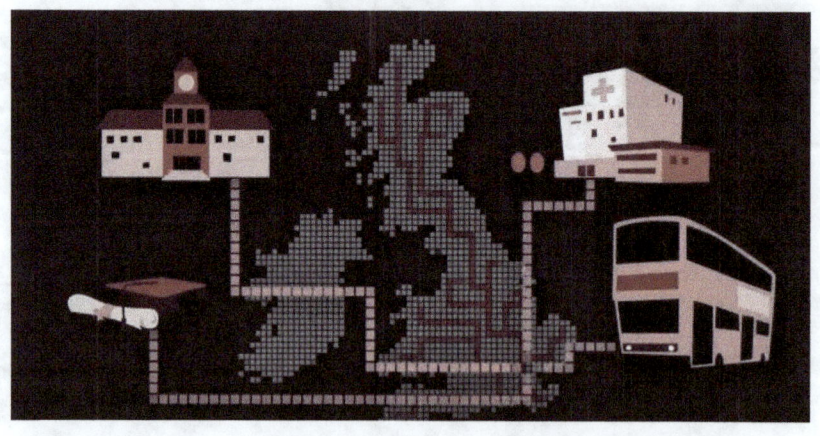

They loan / fund all areas of sector with Debt!

They gamble and manipulate the markets at depositors' money!

They inflate markets artificially!

FRACTIONAL RESERVE BANKING

EVIL SYSTEM OF RIBA (USURY)!

This mechanism allows the banks to maintain certain percentage (generally 10% of totals depositors funds / currency and use the rest to do business like loaning etc. and generate handsome profits from the funds, which **do not belong to them!** In case majority of people decide to withdraw their currency, there will be not enough funds available with them and **banks will go "default"**. Hence, they are doing business without any solid foundation and indebting the masses, who works day and night to pay their debts plus the interest charged by these blood sucking monsters!

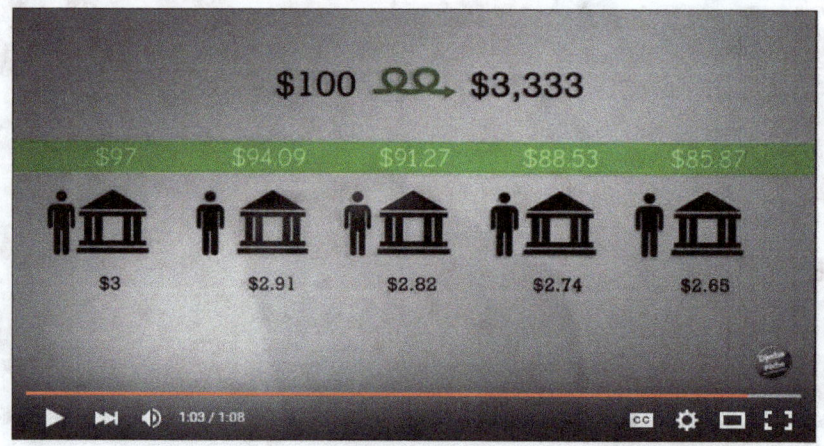

MONEY MULTIPLIER: E.g. EVERY $10 CAN MULTIPLY TO $100 & GOES TO ENORMOUS NUMBERS

WARNING! - A MATEHEMATICAL IMPOSSIBILITY

The Ever-Increasing <u>Loan (Debt) + Interest</u> will never be possible to pay-off in any economy!

GDP can never be equal to National Debt + Interest

(IMPOSSIBLE FOR ALMOST ANY ECONOMY NOWADAYS!!!)

RESULT

POSSIBLE SCENARIOS OF FINANCIAL BUBBLES

About to

HENCE, THIS EVIL, FRAUD, LUDICROUS SYSTEM CHALLENGES TWO ATTRIBUTES OF ALLAH SWT (THE ONE LORD GOD)

AL MUBDI (THE ONE WHO CREATES OUT OF NOTHING)

AND

AL RAZZAQ (THE SUSTAINER, THE PROVIDER WITHOUT ANY LIMITATION)

HOW MORTGAGE SYSTEM WORKS?

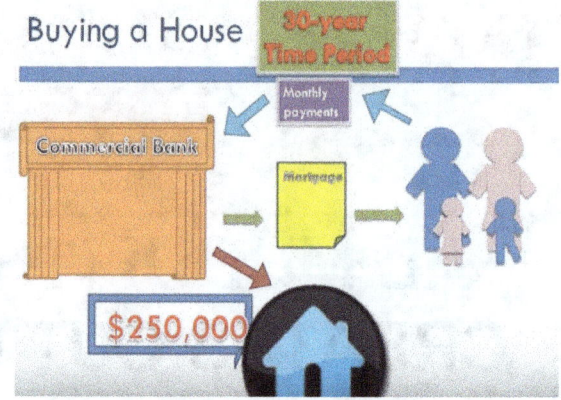

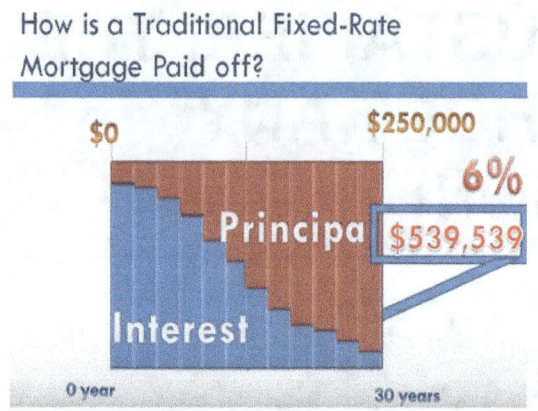

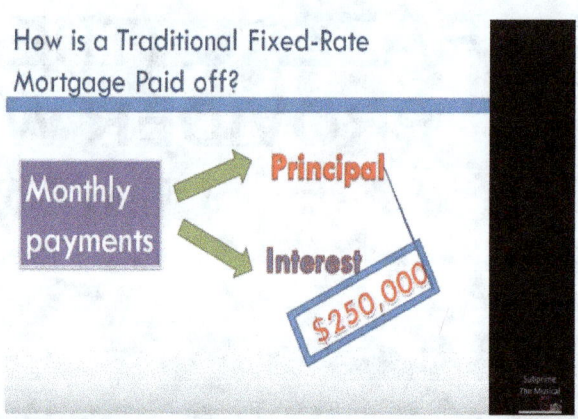

IT CAN BE CLEARLY SEEN THAT THIS SYSTEM CHARGES MORE THAN TWICE OVER THE PERIOD OF TIME DUE TO CHARGING INTEREST (USURY), EASY INCOME GENERATION CREATED OUT OF NOTHING!!!

INTERNATIONAL MONETARY SYSTEM

WHAT IS THE DIFFERENCE BETWEEN CURRENCY AND MONEY?

This question is of **prime importance** but majority of the people, even those who are qualified in the fields of economics, finance and accounts are unfortunately unaware of the basic difference between "**Currency and Money**" and it's a **reality**, therefore we can very well imagine the ignorance of the masses!

CURRENCY:

Anything, which can be used as a:

- ✓ Medium of Exchange
- ✓ Method of Accounting
- ✓ Divisible
- ✓ Durable
- ✓ Fungible
- ✓ Portable

E.G.

- Paper Currency (Fiat Currency), Digital Currency – No Value of its own, rather "Fictitious Value associated to it"!

MONEY:

Anything, which can be used as a:

- ✓ Medium of Exchange
- ✓ Method of Accounting
- ✓ Divisible
- ✓ Durable
- ✓ Fungible
- ✓ Portable
- ✓ **Has Intrinsic Value** i.e. the "**Value is within the money**"

E.G.

- **Precious metals like "Gold, Silver Coins" or other commodities can be used as means of exchange for goods / services** (in the absence or shortage of precious metals in the market)

The system based on "**money**" has been in use by mankind for around **5,000 years**, until recently (after the creation of Federal Reserve Bank 1913), restricted (eventually) from being used in the market. Rather, the paper fiat currency completely replaced the "money", for the ulterior motives, which we will explain ahead. Now, nobody can even think of using the "money i.e. **gold and silver coins**" for exchange of goods!

TRANSFORMATION OF MONETARY SYSTEMS

The monetary system transformed from **Pure Gold / Silver Standard** - Real Money (before the creation of Federal Reserve Bank in 1913), then switched over to Gold Exchange Standard (will be explained ahead), then to "Petro-Dollar Standard" and now planned to "Central Bank Digital Currency". **Paper will be eliminated completely! Then the authorities will be able to trace, track and monitor each an every transaction of the user and be able to dictate their authority to masses!**

Since, everyone is bound to use "currency" for the daily needs, so in case anyone gets out of the line or disagrees with the authority, their "digital wallet" can be blocked and enslaved very easily!

A SHOCKING, BUT NEGLECTED REALITY UNAWARE BY THE MAJORITY!

Since, we have defined "money" explicitly, therefore it will be now easy for the reader to comprehend, why the **founding fathers of USA** drafted the Constitution and mentioned **money** below:

ARTICLE I (US CONSTITUTION) LEGISLATIVE BRANCH

SECTION 10 POWERS DENIED STATES
Clause 1 Proscribed Powers

- No State shall enter into any Treaty, Alliance, or Confederation; grant Letters of Marque and Reprisal; **coin Money**; emit Bills of Credit; **make any Thing but gold and silver Coin a Tender in Payment of Debts**; pass any

Bill of Attainder, ex post facto Law, or Law impairing the Obligation of Contracts, or grant any Title of Nobility.

There is no provision in the Constitution to use any type of "fake, fiat, paper currency other than Gold and Silver in the market !

That's why:

Henry Ford once said, "It is well enough that people of the nation do not understand our banking and monetary system, for if they did, I believe there would be a revolution before tomorrow morning".

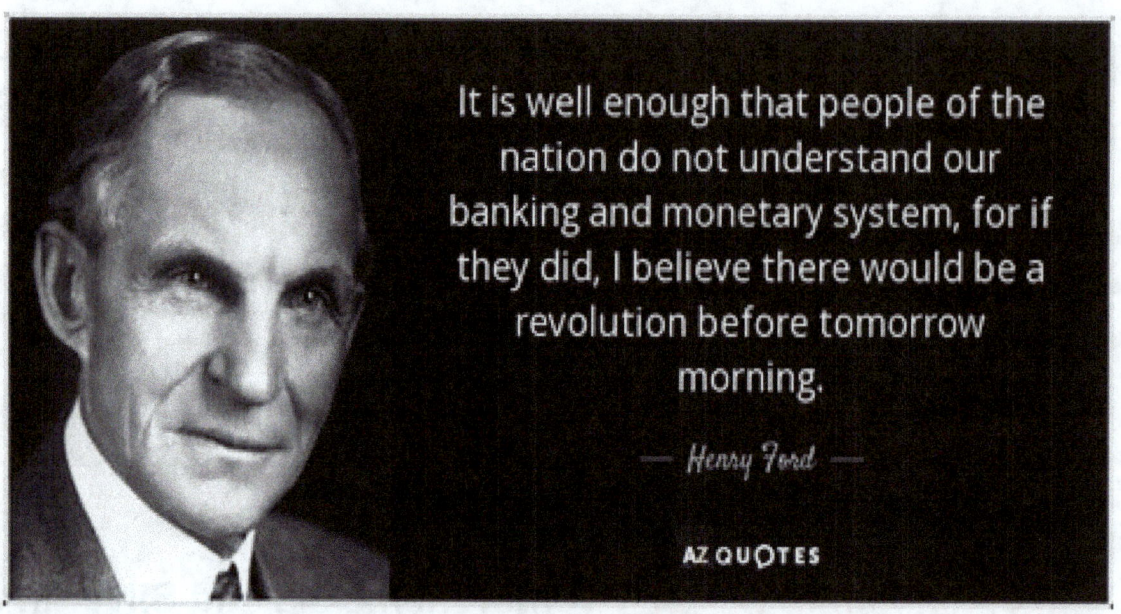

It is well enough that people of the nation do not understand our banking and monetary system, for if they did, I believe there would be a revolution before tomorrow morning.

— Henry Ford —

AZ QUOTES

WHY WAS "REAL MONEY" REPLACED WITH "FIAT CURRENCY"?

- **Federal Reserve Bank** (Privately owned) was created in 1913

- **1 Ounce of gold = USD 20** (Paper Currency)

- **April 1933, the US Government enacted legislation** at that time prohibiting (UNCONSTITUTIONAL) American residents from **keeping gold coins** (CONSTITUTIONAL), bullion, or gold certificates in their possession – **Prohibition of Gold / Silver usage as money by the common people** but can redeem their currency in gold.

- **January 1934**, the US Government devalued the US paper dollar by **41% 1 Ounce of gold = USD 35** (thus ripped-off the masses officially, by a legalized theft, courtesy "**devaluation of currency**", as they could have never been able to do in case of **money**, because it is real metal and **cannot be printed or created out of thin air!** The journey to enslave humanity and moving them toward destitution by the blood sucking bankers began!!!

The **Federal Reserve Bank** appeared in the above incident to have initiated a '**trial run**' to **test domestically the new monetary system** through which a **massive and unjust transfer of wealth throughout the unsuspecting world could be achieved**. That transfer would take place through the simple device of creating money out of worthless paper and then forcing paper currency upon all of mankind. Those who control the monetary system would then target certain currencies and force them to be continuously devalued. **As such paper currencies lost value the unsuspecting masses would suffer massive loss of wealth, however, their 'losses would result in 'gain' for others.**

September 1931, the **British pound** was devalued by **30%** and this gradually increased to **40% by 1934**. **France** then devalued **French Franc by 30%,** the **Italian Lira was devalued by 41%,** and the **Swiss Franc by 30%.** The same thing subsequently happened in most European countries. Only **Greece** went beyond the rest of Europe to **devalue** its currency by a **whopping 59%.** This led to Great Depression!

In other words, the Great Depression was artificially engineered to justify the imposition of a new international monetary system that would bring order to a chaotic world of money!!

The **Bretton Woods Agreement** (fig leaf) paved the way for the **International Monetary Fund to be established in 1944** with the explicit function of maintaining an **international monetary system** of precisely such **non-redeemable paper currencies.**

At this forum it was decided that "**only governments (state level) can redeem their currencies in gold,** since the **paper USD** was

assumed to be <u>gold backing</u>, no individual will be allowed to redeem his possession of "paper currency into "gold"!! Although written on "currency notes", but it is all fraud! – Hence, "paper currency" turned 99.99% fake / fraud!!

By 1971 even the fig leaf disappeared when **USA "broke its promise"** on its <u>treaty obligation under international law to redeem US dollars for gold,</u> when **French President Charles De Gaulle** approached President Nixon for the redemption of **USD 2 billion** into **"gold"**. USA blatantly denied that, although they had promised but they are under no obligation to fulfil their promise, hence goodbye to any sort of sanctity to **utterly fraud, fake, fiat** and now <u>100% fraud paper currency (USD)!!!</u>

EMERGENCE OF PETRO-DOLLAR!

In 1973, US Secretary of State Henry Kissinger convinced the late King Faisal to "sell their oil for only US Dollars". All other Arab nations (OPEC) followed Saudi Arabia. Thereafter, USD became the most practical currency for buying and selling the mostly demanded commodity in the world, thus giving USD the status of "world reserve currency" and monopoly to any competition. This gave USA the power import oil for free, as the Fed Reserve Bank could print as much notes as it liked to meet the demands its people, "out of thin air", besides doing much else as well.

This was the ultimate goal of taking <u>real money</u> out of the market and replacing it with fake, fraud, and utterly oppressive <u>paper currency</u>!

FUTURE OF CURRENCY

As mentioned above "money" the **real form of wealth created by our One Lord God Allah SWT** had been transformed into **fake / fraud / fiat / haram** "paper currency" with the passage of time, <u>not for the benefit of humanity but for controlling them!</u>

It is **impossible to manipulate and amass infinite wealth**, had the "money" (gold / silver / precious metals /commodities) **was in use for the transactions.** Further the **mankind would have been quite saved from the monster of "inflation",** which is dangerous than a "nuclear bomb", as it <u>can destroy the economies and take the population into destitution within 'no time'</u>. This is the core objective of this evil "transformation" by the bankers of the world!

Now, they have planned to **eliminate the fake / fiat "paper currency "**from the market and move toward "Central Bank Digital Currency" to have **<u>full spectrum domination</u>** over mankind and resources!

GLOBAL RULING ELITE - PYRAMID

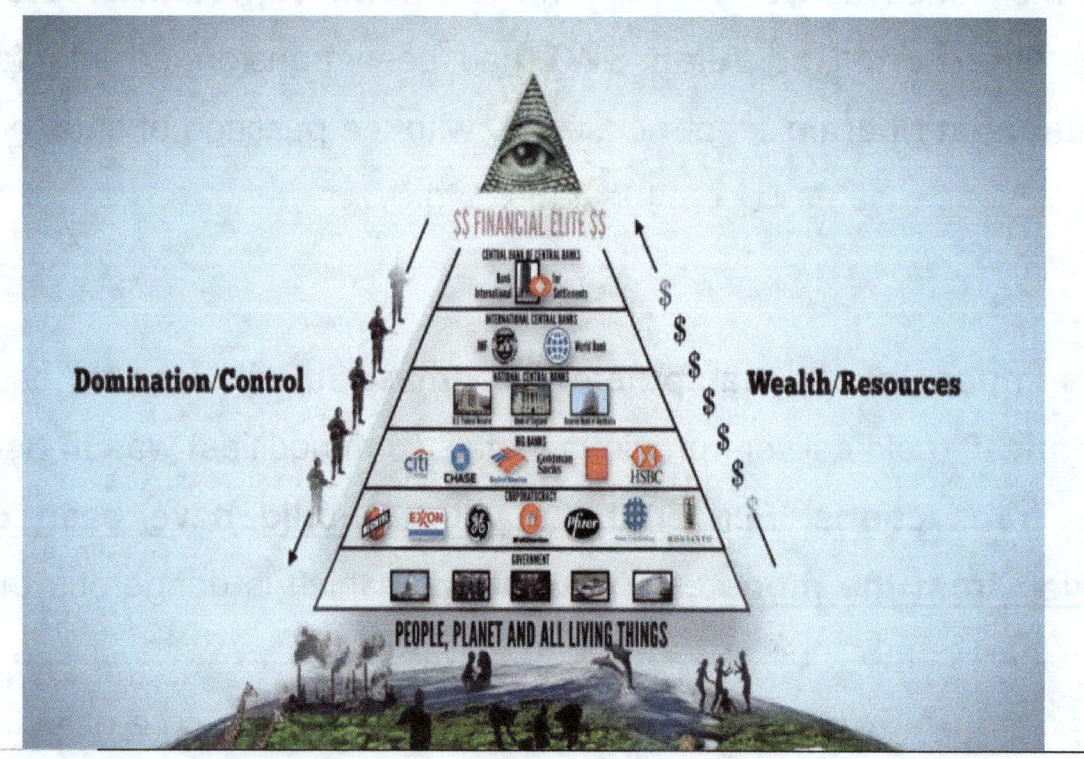

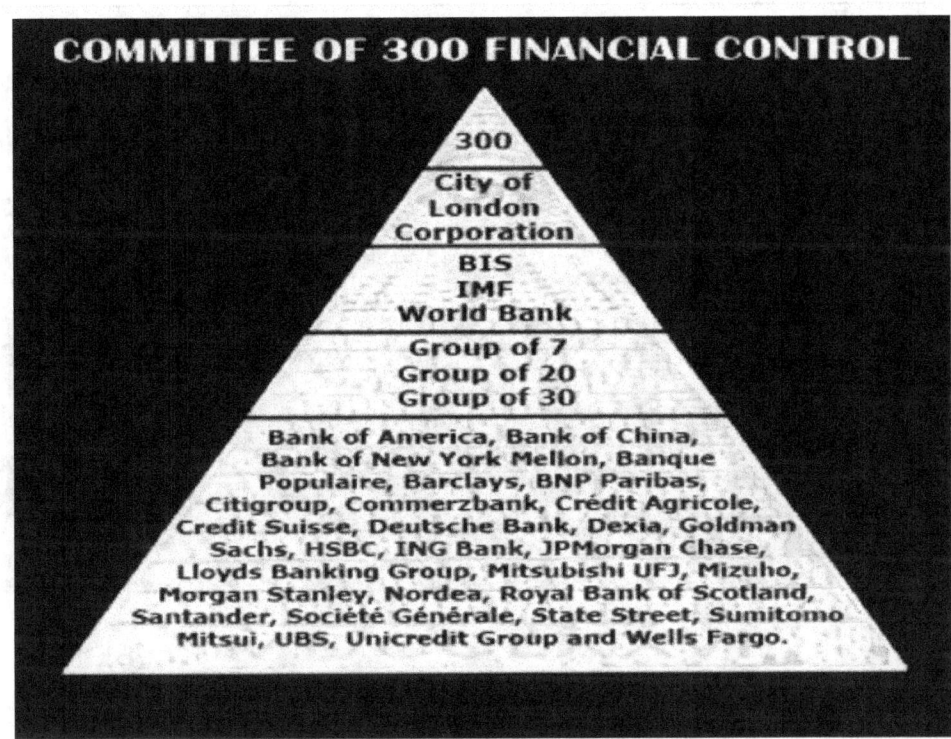

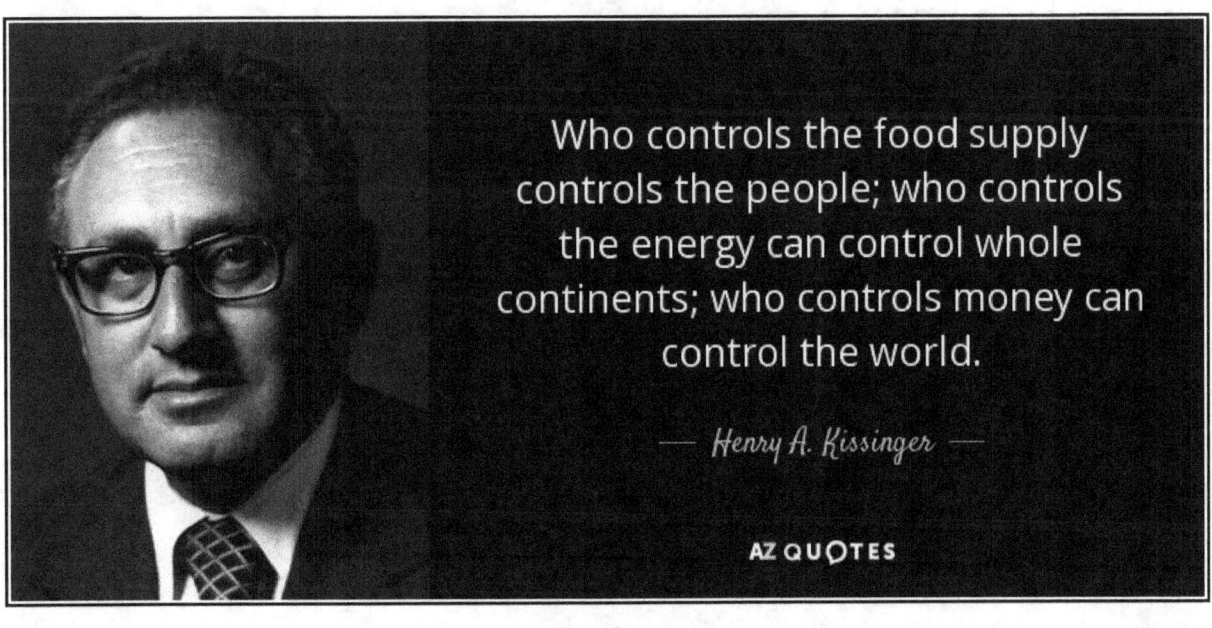

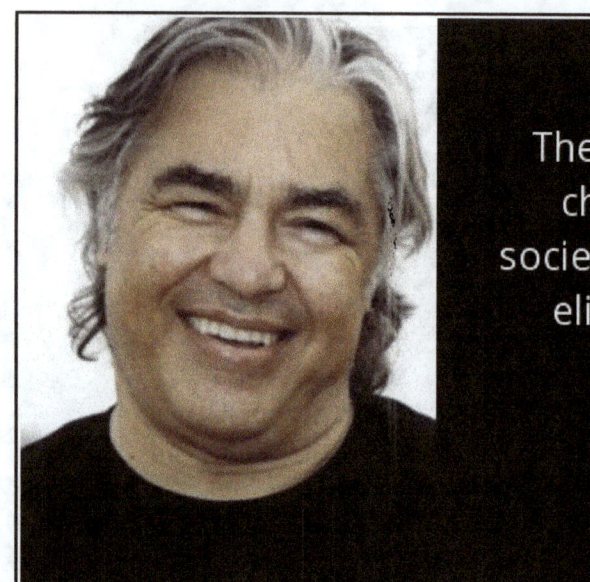

The end goal is to get everybody chipped, to control the whole society, to have the bankers and the elite people control the world.

— Aaron Russo —

AZ QUOTES

WHAT IS SECULARISM?

- **The belief that religion should not be involved in the organization of society, education, etc. – Oxford Dictionary**

- **The attitude that religion should have no place in civil affairs – Collins Dictionary**

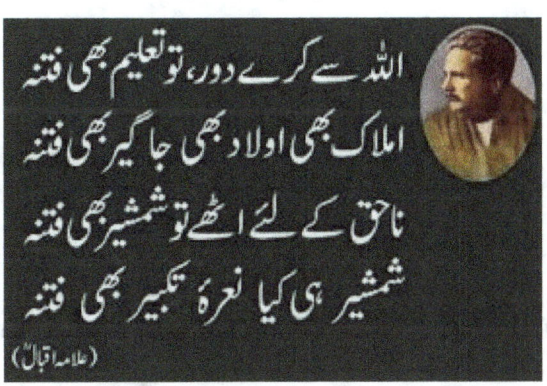

اللہ سے کرے دور، تو تعلیم بھی فتنہ

املاک بھی اولاد بھی جاگیر بھی فتنہ

ناحق کے لئے اٹھے تو شمشیر بھی فتنہ

شمشیر ہی کیا نعرۂ تکبیر بھی فتنہ

(علامہ اقبالؒ)

وِیں ہاتھ سے دے کر اگر آزاد ہو ملت

ہے ایسی تجارت میں سلماں کا خسارا

ISLAMIC PERSPECTIVE

DEFINITIONS OF RIBA (USURY)

➢ 'An addition to, or an increase of a thing over its size or amount'

➢ 'Increase (profit) at the expense of the wealth of other' - (Holy Quran, 30: 39)

➢ **'Consuming wealth of mankind through means false and wrong (baatil) -** (Holy Quran, 4: 161)

Comments:

'Increase in capital, at the expense of the wealth of others, through means which are false & wrong'

'Any unlawful addition, by way of interest to a sum of money or goods lent by one person or body of persons to another'

This is irrespective of the rate of interest & the motivation involved. It is sometimes difficult to recognize Riba because it is often disguised as legalized theft.

❖ Riba (Interest) is not business, rather oppression! Riba (Interest) is Haram , while business is Halal (legal.

There must be element of <u>risk, of profit or loss</u>, in a <u>free & fair market</u>. In Riba, this free and fair <u>market is bypassed with no element of risk, no loss & only profit can occur.</u>

MONEY IN ISLAM

Abī Sa'īd al-Khudri reported Allah's Messenger Muhammad (peace be upon him and his progeny) as saying: "<u>Gold for gold, silver for silver, wheat for wheat, barley for barley, dates for dates, and salt for salt,</u> (when a transaction is) like for like, payment being made on the spot, then if anyone <u>gives more or asks for more</u>, he has

dealt in Riba (Interest / Usury), the receiver and the giver being equally guilty." - (Sahīh, Muslim)

Money is located within Allah's creation with value assigned to it i.e. value is within the money (intrinsic) by The One Lord God Himself, Who is the Creator of wealth!!

Allah SWT is Al Mubdi and Al Razzaq

EVILS OF RIBA (USURY)!

Losses in Religiosity and the Hereafter	A notice of War From Allah (SWT) and His Messenger (SAWS)	The most heinous practicable sin!	Deprivation of Allah's (SWT)Mercy	Damned and Cursed by the Prophet (SAWS)

	The Punishment of Hellfire with serpents in the belly	Dispossession of Jannat	Rejection of all Supplications	Rejection of all Worships
Losses in the Worldly / Material Life	Negative impact on investment	Disregard to Hard Work	Ownership on the bread earned by others	Egocentricity and Self-interest Exorbitant Profiteering
	Burden of Regressive Taxes	Disruption in the fair circulation of wealth Control of Capitalists	Oppression of the workers	Increase in Inflation and Unemployment

PROHIBITION OF RIBA IN QURAN AND SUNNAH (TRADITIONS)

QURANIC VERSES:

- "Those who devour riba shall not stand on the Day of Judgement, but like the standing of one whom the Shaytan (Satan) has made by touch "– Al Baqara:275

- "O Believers! Fear Allah and <u>leave what remains of riba</u> if you are Muslims." – Al Baqara:278

- "But if you do not like this, then <u>take notice of war from Allah SWT and the Messenger of Allah.</u> And if you repent, then take your principal sums, neither you wring any one or be wronged yourselves – Al Baqara:279

TRADITIONS:

- "Avoid the seven greatest destructive sins. Riba is one of them." – Sahih Bukhari

- **The Messenger of Allah (SWT)** "cursed the one who consumes riba and the one who pays it, the one who writes it down (records transactions) and the two witnesses it, and he added: they are all same (in sin) "– Abu Daud

- "Riba is of seventy different parts (degrees of sin), the least heinous being equivalent to a man marrying (i.e. sexual intercourse his own mother" – Abu Daud

FREE AND FAIR MARKET

Islam believes in a Free and Fair Market and for this system to be established the following are necessary:

- **Freedom of access to the market**

- **Freedom of competition in the market**

- **Freedom of the market to determine its own prices (i.e. there must be no fixed prices, no minimum wages etc.)**

- **Freedom to produce anything for the market (but must be Halal, really Shariah compliant!)**

- **Freedom to buy & sell anything Halal in the market**

- **Prohibition against stealing and cheating e.g. under-weighing items for sale or for that matter "legalized theft"**

- **If there is no free and fair market, this will lead to mischief in the land, and due to the Riba / Usury /Interest based Economy resulting in market being unfair!!**

PROHIBITION OF MORTGAGES IN WESTERN SOCIETY

It has been one of the sensitive and serious issues for the Muslims settled in the Western societies that whether buying the houses through mortgages offered by the conventional / Islamic banks and financial institutions are "**Valid /Halal**" or "**In-valid / Haram**". Since, these types of contracts involve Interest (Riba), which is strictly forbidden in Quran by Allah S.W.T, therefore demands **serious and careful study** from the "**Fiqh**" (Islamic Shariah) perspective in an objective manner.

BACKGROUND

A Fatwah (religious / Shariah ruling) was issued in November 1999 (Rajab 1420 Hijri) after a Fiqh (Shariah) debate that took over in the **European Council for Fatwa and Research**, while a second Fatwa was issued three weeks later in Sha'ban 1420 Hijri (1998) by the **League of Shariah Scholars of North America** in a conference held in Detroit, Michigan. These Fatwahs concluded in **permitting buying houses in the Western Societies thorough interest (Riba) based mortgages**.

These Fatwah led to the **confusion in the minds** of the Muslims because they were challenged by the renowned Islamic scholars not only within the said conferences but across the world. Related to the subject, we can broadly categorize the Muslims, pursuing for buying the houses in **three categories:**

a) Those who have already decided and buying houses on mortgages (without looking for any Fatwa / Islamic Ruling/ alternative).

b) Those who are very clear in their minds and know that Riba is "Haram / Forbidden" in **every type and in any part of the world.** It is a major sin (i.e., waging war with Allah S.W.T. and His Messenger Muhammad S.A.W.S.) and they **are not going to approach this major sin for buying their houses in any case!**

c) **People who are confused and looking for alternative / solution / Islamic Ruling** (with **solid references** from Quran and Sunnah) through **trustworthy Ulama** (Islamic scholars) and are in the middle of way for deciding either way.

Our humble effort is basically focused on the **third category**. For this we will rely on the book written by a world renown Islamic scholar **Dr. Salah Al Sawi**, published in 1999 (after the issuance of above-mentioned Fatwah) titled (translated from Arabic) as "Polite Reconsideration of the Fatwa permitting Riba Based Loans for

Home Mortgages in the West", which is available online in PDF format for referencing.

THE PREMISES FROM FIQH FOR THOSE WHO PERMIT INTEREST BASED MORTGAGES!

These declarations were based on treating need (hajah) like necessity (darurah) in **allowing the forbidden** or relying on the **position of Imam Abu Hanifa and his student Muhammad al-Shaybani, viz. the view that dealing in riba is allowed in** dar al-harb **(living in an enemy state).**

- **What is attributed to Imam Abu Hanifa and some other people of knowledge, of the permissibility of dealing via invalid contracts in dar al-harb, including dealing in riba.** Note that the final conference declaration of the **League of Sharia Scholars does not mention** this premise, although its academic papers and Fiqh discussions clearly included it, as opposed to the concluding

51

declaration of the European **Council for Ifta' and Research, which includes a clear mention of this premise in its text.**

- **The principle of treating need similarly to necessity in allowing the forbidden.** Since a home is **one of the necessary needs** which must be met, either by renting or ownership, and since renting leads to many undesirable consequences, there is a general need for Muslims in this land to partake in this arrangement. **This ensures an overall benefit and repels the overall harms;** hence the view that usurious loans are allowed in order to ensure these benefits and repel these harms.

- **What is connected to the previous principle and established in Fiqh, that whatever is prohibited as a means towards evil may be allowed out of need, while whatever is intrinsically prohibited can only be permitted out of necessity.** Since what is intrinsically prohibited is the devouring of riba, that is what is only permitted out of necessity, but those things that lead to that, such as paying riba or writing or witnessing the contract, are prohibited as a means towards evil, so they are permitted out of need.

- **That the Muslim is not obliged under the Sharia to establish Islamic civil, financial and political law and other such matters which are related to the general system, in a society which does not accept Islam, since this is not within his capability. The prohibition of riba is one of these rulings which is related to the essential nature of the society and to the philosophy of the state and its social and economic orientation.** Rather, the Muslim is required to establish the rulings which concern him personally such as those of ritual worship, food, drink and dress, and those related to marriage, divorce, remarriage, 'iddah, inheritance and other personal matters. These are such that if these matters **are constrained for him**, and he is not able to establish his religion in them in any way, it becomes obligatory for him to migrate within Allah's spacious earth as soon as he finds a way to do so.

- **The consequences of not dealing with these invalid contracts, including Riba, in Dar al-harb, i.e. that a Muslim's holding fast to Islam becomes a cause of his economic weakness and financial loss,** whereas the basic principle is that Islam strengthens a person and does not weaken him, increases him in prosperity and does not decrease him, and benefits him and does not harm him.

- **The overall benefits which will result from the permissibility of owning houses in this way: protection of one's religion and Islamic personality, improvement of the Muslims' living conditions and liberation from the economic shackles upon them.** Thus they will be able to fulfil the obligation of da'wah and take part in building the society at large, such that their level will rise. They will then deserve to be called the best nation brought forth for mankind, and will become a radiant image of Islam in front of the non-Muslims

AUTHENTIC ISLAMIC RESPONSE FROM DR. SALAH AL SAWI

In order to gain in depth knowledge (Ilm) on the subject matter and be able to find "**Truth**", please find the links of **five videos** uploaded on **YouTube**, which are the easy explanation to the book referred above under the headings:

Fiqh Debate: Part1 Interest based Mortgages for buying homes in Western Societies: https://youtu.be/mnffNN4iPZI

Fiqh Debate (under same heading): Part 2:
https://youtu.be/Efdq74av8CM

Fiqh Debate: Part 3: https://youtu.be/iswGKsvetUI

Fiqh Debate: Part 4: https://youtu.be/nl0-X1qAykk

Fiqh Debate: Part 5: https://youtu.be/Mo-k-Gr2JuY

The above videos / explanation are simplified and summarized form (to save some time) about the response from Dr. Salah Al Sawi to the Fatwah, **permitting Buying houses on Mortgages,** so that the reader may be able to judge in an objective manner whether is it really "**Halal / Valid**" or "Haram / In-Valid" to go for mortgages in the Western societies?

CONSIDERATION FOR ENGAGING IN MORTGAGE CONTRACTS

Kindly consider:

- **Qarz e Hasna (A soft loan without any interest /usury)**
- **Profit**
- **Promise**

Please bear in mind that the above mentioned, if **treated individually** are **valid and noble concepts**, but if these "**three**" are **combined** in one "**Contract**" will be declared as "**Riba / In-Valid**". In order to consider any mortgage / Loan contract, please be advised to consider as follows:

✓ **Check if the Bank / Loaning Agency will have the <u>ownership</u> of the property during the Contract?**

✓ **If the Bank / Loaning Agency has the ownership of the property, then check whether all <u>sorts of maintenance cost and insurance should be borne by the Bank / Loaning Agency</u>.**

The borrower should not bear any sort of liability (in case of

zero ownership) or bear only according to its share **(in case of Mudarabah) per Contract, otherwise it will be not Shariah Compliant!**

✓ The **Bank / Loaning Agency** <u>MUST finalize / agree upon the total cost</u> **of the property before making the Agreement / Disbursement of funds to the buyer** for the purchase of property. **E.g.** The buyer wishes to buy a house worth **£300,000/-** through the Bank / Agency, then both parties must agree at the said price and say, **20 years period of instalments** beforehand. The buyer agrees to pay the down-payment worth **£10,000/-.** Now the balance amount **(£290,000/- as financing)** will be divided as: **290,000/240 = £1,250/- per month** [Nothing should be hidden and irrespective of any sort of rates / interest fluctuations by the Central Bank – Riba free!] – This will be a valid transaction, In shaa Allah **(Wa Allah o Aalam).**

RULE: <u>**CASH OR CREDIT TRANSACTION MUST HAVE SAME VALUE**</u>

NO QUESTION OF TIME VALUE OF MONEY (ANY SORT OF ADDITONAL AMOUNT CHARGED BY THE LENDER) IN A SHARIAH BASED CONTRACT!

POSSIBLE SOLUTIONS TO AVOID MORTGAGE CONTRACTS FOR HOUSING OWNERSHIP

- **Pooling of funds** in a Muslim community for buying a piece of land (preferably away from main cities) and building reasonable / standard size accommodation for the families – **Dr. Bilal Philips implemented solution within his community in Canada**

- **A coordinated campaigning** for encouraging the **wealthy and God conscious people** for providing Qarz e hasna (loan without interest) with soft repayment schedule to the needy. Establishment of **confidence and sincerity (taqwa) is must for both parties**!

- In a community, move-out toward countryside (rural) to purchase cheap land and **establish Muslim model villages** - live a simple life and **establish Dar ul Islam** (Muslim community on a limited scale), under one Ameer (leader). This will also help in preserving the "Faith" in the current age of Fitan (trials and tribulations), as we are living in **End Times!**

- People **may engage with the financial institutions**, who offer to invest and **mutually share the ownership and risk of the property.** They should and device a mechanism that does not involve Riba, rather the institution may earn their returns via "**Rental Income**" from the buyer and **eventually transfer the ownership rights to the buyer** in a period on mutually agreed basis. No exploitation to any party, **rather a fair business transaction!**

CONVENTIONAL AND ISLAMIC BANKING SYSTEMS IN PAKISTAN – A CASE STUDY

A BRIEF HISTORY OF STRUGGLE AGAINST RIBA IN PAKISTAN

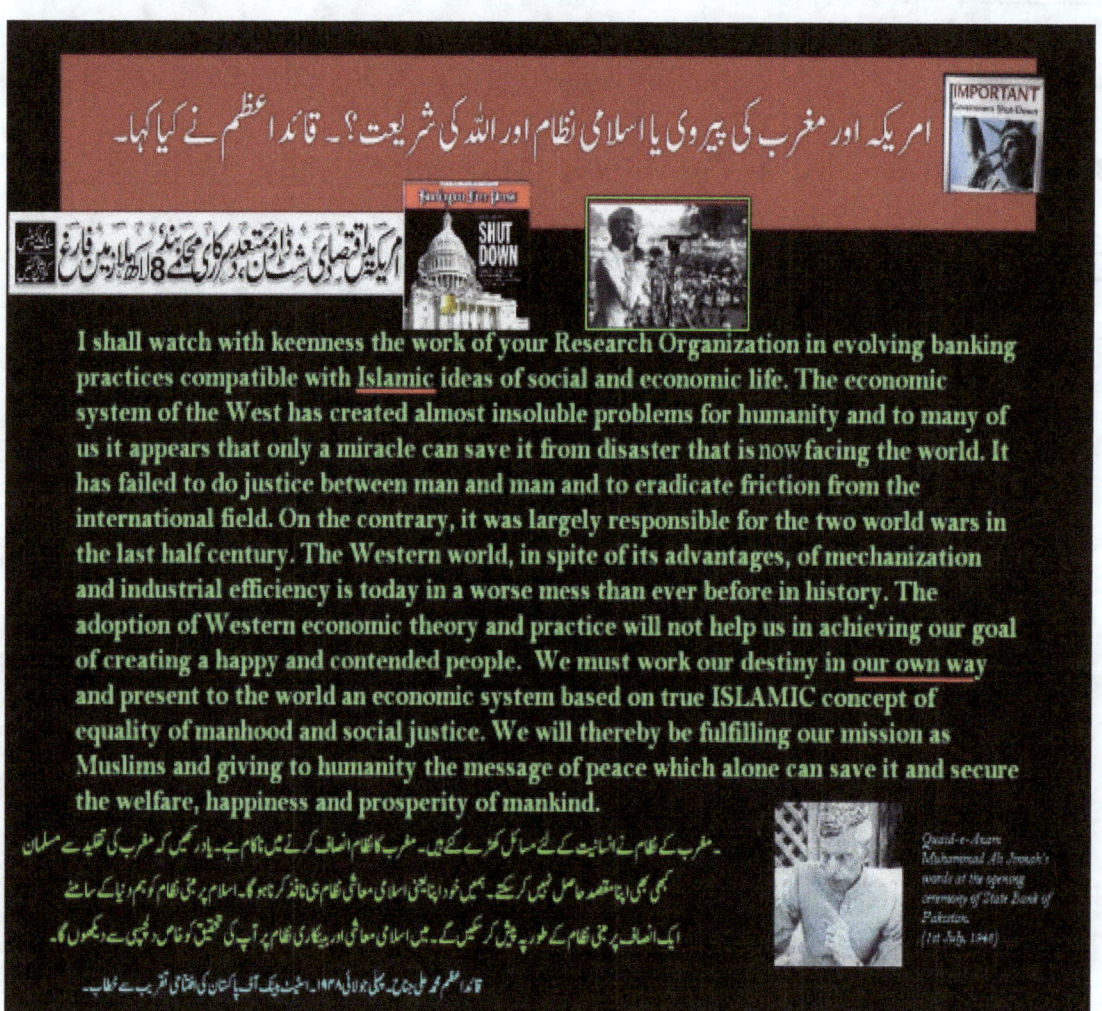

I shall watch with keenness the work of your Research Organization in evolving banking practices compatible with Islamic ideas of social and economic life. The economic system of the West has created almost insoluble problems for humanity and to many of us it appears that only a miracle can save it from disaster that is now facing the world. It has failed to do justice between man and man and to eradicate friction from the international field. On the contrary, it was largely responsible for the two world wars in the last half century. The Western world, in spite of its advantages, of mechanization and industrial efficiency is today in a worse mess than ever before in history. The adoption of Western economic theory and practice will not help us in achieving our goal of creating a happy and contended people. We must work our destiny in our own way and present to the world an economic system based on true ISLAMIC concept of equality of manhood and social justice. We will thereby be fulfilling our mission as Muslims and giving to humanity the message of peace which alone can save it and secure the welfare, happiness and prosperity of mankind.

Quaid-e-Azam Muhammad Ali Jinnah's words at the opening ceremony of State Bank of Pakistan. (1st July, 1948)

- **1969 – The Islamic Consultation Council** proclaimed Saving Certificates and Prize Bonds etcetera to be kinds of Riba!

- **1973 – It was declared in <u>Article 38 of Constitution</u> that** immediate eradication of transactions involving in giving and taking "riba" **was the State obligation of the government of Pakistan**

- **1977 – The Council of Islamic Ideology was delegated the responsibility to design and propose recommendations for creating an <u>alternative, non-riba based Economic System</u>**

- **1980 – The Council of Islamic Ideology published its final report.**

- **1981 – The Federal Sharia Court was established**

- **1988 – An Islamic Economic Commission was established with the promulgation of the implementation of the Sharia Ordinance**

- **1991 – The Federal Sharia Court declared "bank interest" as Riba / Usury!**

- **1991 – The government of Pakistan filed appeal in the Supreme Court of Pakistan against the decision made by Federal Sharia Court, no hearing took place until 1999**

- **1997 – The then Prime Minister (Nawaz Sharif), along with his father and brother met with Dr. Israr Ahmad (late) at Qur'an Academy Lahore. Late Dr. Israr Ahmad directed their attention toward the abolishment of "Riba", which they promised to abolish "very soon"**

- **1997 – The government of Pakistan made another committee to abolish riba from the country.**

- **1999 – The Supreme Court of Pakistan upholds and ratifies the decision made by the Federal Sharia Court on riba.**

- **2001 – The government of Pakistan used UBL to file an appeal in the Supreme Court of Pakistan requesting "further time" to consider the implementation of the decision. Delay tactics!**

- **2015 – The Supreme Court of Pakistan dismissed the petition for the "abolition of riba (usury / bank interest) filed by Ameer e Tanzeem e Islami, Hafiz Akif Saeed dated October 6, 2015, remarking that "...whomsoever do not want to take riba, ought not and whomsoever do, Allah will ask of them (i.e. accountable)". Subhan Allah!!**

- **2022 – The Federal Sharia Court (FSC) on Thursday announced a verdict in a long-pending case on Riba (interest), declaring the prevailing interest-based banking system as against the Sharia and directed the government to facilitate all loans under an interest-free system - Source: https://www.dawn.com/news/1687237**

BANKING SYSTEM IN PAKISTAN – AT A GLANCE!

- According to State Bank of Pakistan, there are 30.88 million accounts holders in the Banking System. 88% are with Conventional Banks, while 12% are with Islamic Banks

- 3.2 million people were given loans out of 200 million population!

- 30,000 individuals / organizations took loans worth Rs.3,000 billion (concentration of wealth!)

- Savings Accounts received average profit worth 4%, while Banks shareholders earned 22% profit!!, majority is exploited!!!

- 2001 – Banks earning was Rs. 1 billion and they use to give 6.5% to their depositors. In 2015, they earned Rs. 247 billion (combined) and gave the depositors just 4% (peanuts)!!

- Huge Loans worth billions are being write-off! Oppression and exploitation!!

- Majority of governments earning goes in Debt Servicing (local & foreign). Rs 1.542 trillion (6.7 % of GDP) of interest paid to its local and foreign debtors during the last fiscal year, FY13. Every individual in Pakistan is under debt over Rs. 200,000 approx. (off-course un-willingly!)

ISLAMIC BANKING SYSTEM

CORE OBJECTIVES OF ISLAMIC BANKING SYSTEM

- There should <u>not be</u> an "iota" of "Interest / Riba" involved in such system

- The evils of "Riba" <u>must be eradicated</u>, otherwise it is of no utility

- It should <u>support the Islamic Economic System</u> in a gradual manner

ISLAMIC BANKING SYSTEM IN PAKISTAN – BOMBSHELLS!

- Current, Islamic Banking System, managed by the Ulema / Muftis (religious scholars) have never claimed to achieve the previously mentioned objectives mentioned above!

- One of the leading Mufti Taqi Usmani has accepted (off the record) while discussing with Dr. Shahid Siddiqui "this Islamic Banking System is un-Islamic"

- Further, some ulemma on a live TV talk show (debate), agreed with Dr. Shahid Siddiqui (Economist) that current Islamic Banking System cannot be said as "Islamic".

- 2001 – Al Meezan Bank was the first Islamic Bank in Pakistan

- The current Islamic Banking System is an eye-washer to the "God-fearing" masses to provide them with an alternative and nothing else!!! In actual practice it is same as conventional banking!!

- **Sep. 4, 2001 – Gen. Pervez Musharraf Regime: In a meeting comprising of top Scholar (Shariah Judge), Governor State Bank, Member of Islamic Ideology Council and President Pervez, <u>agreed to pass an Order that they will run two parallel Banking System for the people as per their choice</u> – Subhan Allah! This is the state of affair of our Ulema!!**

WAIT FOR THE SHOCK!

- **In 2015 State Bank of Pakistan, under the Chairmanship of Mufti Taqi Usmani (Islamic Banking Governing Board) <u>approved a transaction worth Rs. 208 billion</u> (profit transferring to the Islamic Banks only, upon maturity of Sukuk Bonds in possession by the commercial / conventional banks). This is an enormous transfer of funds, which are 100% Interest (Riba)!!**

- Justice Saeed Uz zaman Siddiqui said to Dr. Shahid Siddiqui on a TV show after the judgement by the Supreme Court in 1999, which declared "banking interest is haram", President Pervez Musharraf phoned him and said "....you are doing conspiracy against us for bringing Islam, this will not be done"

- "Current, Marhaba and Ijarah based transactions are interest based (it is Riba from back door) and haram" – Dr. Shahid Siddiqui – A well-known and respectable economist

COMPARISON OF CONVENTIONAL & ISLAMIC BANKING SYSTEMS IN PAKISTAN

Which is the bigger Evil?

Conventional Banking	Islamic Banking
Big Loans / Financing Disbursement- Out of 100, gave 66% to the Elite	77% to the Elite [Responsible of concentration of wealth, violating the Islamic principle]
Loans to Small Business – 6%	3% [Lesser access to small business]
Agriculture Loans to Small Farmers – 6%	0.4% [Lesser access to small and most deserving class]
Consumer Finance – 6%	12% [contributing toward more spending on extravagant / lavish spending, such cars, bikes, A/Cs, luxuries etc.]

Note: All above figures have been reported by the State Bank of Pakistan and quoted live by Dr. Shahid Siddiqui (Economist)

Hence, all indicators prove that "so called Islamic Banking System" is a big "eye-washer" / fraud and Haram!!!

ISLAMIC RESPONSE

INDIVIDUAL LEVEL – MUSLIMS / MANKIND

- Tauba ul Nasooh (Sincere Repentance) and abstaining from all sorts of Direct Riba transactions not limited to: Housing Mortgage, Murabaha, Ijara, Leasing (involving Interest), Credit Cards, Riba / Interest based Loans, Student Loans, Life Insurance (Fixed Rate of Returns), Stock Exchange Gambling i.e. Dealing in Futures Contract / Derivatives etc.

- Be sincere practicing Muslims / Believer, develop Taqwa (God consciousness) as much as possible for the will and pleasure of Allah SWT and squeeze worldly desires!

OUR DUTY ACCORDING TO QURAN: "You [Muslims] are the best nation brought out for Mankind, commanding what is righteous and forbidding what is wrong." - Al Quran (3:110)

- Be a part of community for an organized struggle in eradicating Riba from Pakistan (at least), Fi Sabeel Lillah! This can be a "kaffara" for living under Taghoot (falsehood society)!!

ULEMA'S (SCHOLAR) LEVEL

- Mufti Taqi Usmani should openly declare that current Islamic Banking System is "Un-Islamic", so that no confusion arises in the minds of the masses, who are really looking for alternative!

- Ulema must appreciate the Curse of Riba and strive for Mass Education at all levels of Society!

- Unite for the Jihad (struggle) Fi Sabeel Lillah against eradicating Riba!! - A bitter pill, as they must raise themselves above the curse of "firqa" / "masalik (petty differences amongst them)" and strive fearlessly for the will and pleasure of Allah SWT

GOVERNMENT OF PAKISTAN

- Immediately withdraw its Appeal against the decision given by the Federal Sharia Court!

- All sorts of Interest / Mark-up in case of local loans must be eradicated without any delay, just by stroke of pen!

- Parliament should declare the Banking Interest as Riba and faithfully chalk-out an implementation plan of Islamic Economic System (with a definite time frame, no more procrastination!!), as proposed by the Islamic Ideology Council in their Reports and guidelines (under authority provided in the Constitution!

- Commit serious efforts in introducing gold (dinar) and silver (dirham) – Sunnah Money, as legal tender!

Then, only we (as a Muslim nation) can deserve to seek the blessings from Allah SWT, which will be enormous, In Shaa Allah

CONCLUSION

➢ The Modern Banking and Monetary systems controlling worldwide is deliberately designed to "control (enslave) the humanity (masses) including the resources" and pushing the mankind (majority) toward their dependence and destitution.

➢ These bankers are behind all wars since **Napoleon wars till date,** that include both **World Wars** and definitely planning for the World War III. These psychopaths always funds both sides and reap the benefits, as "War is a profiteering business for them"

➢ All Central Banks (with very few exceptions) are controlled by the **Central Bank of the World** (Bank of International Settlements), which is controlled by the **few devilish families through their cronies and gophers mentioned earlier**, hence these few people control / govern the world monetary system, which is fake, fraudulent, and utterly haram!

➢ The Banking System runs on the fake, fraudulent, utterly haram paper currency (**bloodline of the economy**), which will be soon **digital** (to control the masses) and based on "Interest / Riba / Sood / Usury" and **oppression**.

➢ All governments of the world are heavily indebted **to their Central Banks and International Donors** due to this built-in fraudulent, ludicrous system **designed as a "fig leaf" to enslave humanity!** These governments impose taxes to pay-off their liabilities but will never ever be able to do so, even if they operate on full economy! The result will be the collapse of economies and emergence of new World Order (quite soon) and this is the **Final Goal of these psychopathic Bankers (World Ruling Evil Class!!**

➤ **Islamic Banks** are also controlled by the Central Banks on same fraudulent foundation, hence treating them an alternative (with exceptions to few operational work-around and types of business transactions) is an "eye-washer "to the public!

➤ Kindly do your **savings in "gold / silver coins** (precious metals)" **stocks related to metals and mining companies and land**, as the current "paper currency based monetary system "will eventually collapse, courtesy big wars, inflation, and chaos across the world. The real "money" will **rescue you and your family / friends from inflation**, as it preserves your buying power in any time and situation, while the fraudulent paper currency will evaporate or seized by the bankers!

❖ If the people want there **should be ultimate peace and tranquillity worldwide** then few steps must be taken, which are:

➤ **Free Market practice**

➤ **Fair Market (Zero Tolerance for the Exploiters and Oppressors)**

- Eradicating of Riba / Interest / Usury with Immediate effect!

- Usage of Gold and Silver coins (**sound money / real wealth**) and get rid- off fraud / fake /fiat / haram Paper Currency!

- Use of "Money" will eliminate the greatest issue of "inflation", no printing of currency to infinity, impossibility of attacks on countries "currencies", no monetary oppression / exploitation, no possibility of legalized theft and ultimately NO UNJUSTIFIED WARS, ultimately "Peace in the World"!!

"Mankind's two biggest enemies are the State and the Central Banks" - Jeff Berwick

Jazak Allah Khair (Thanks) for your kind attention and patience!

May Allah accept our sincere efforts, only for His sake and pleasure

Ameen Ya Rab Al A'alameen!

For Your Kind Feedback Please:
ahsenala@gmail.com

In case you agree, please do recommend this Book to your families and friends in shaa Allah (God Willing)